DROLL PRANKS
for RICH BOYS

THE WEALTHY YOUNG GENTLEMAN'S
GUIDE TO HORSEPLAY

By DAN BULLA
Illustrations by ETHAN RILLY

CHRONICLE BOOKS
SAN FRANCISCO

This is a work of fiction. Any resemblance to actual events, locales, or persons living or dead is entirely coincidental. The material that follows was written in jest and should not be regarded as an instruction manual. Use common sense, abstain from foolish behavior, and no matter how droll it might seem to you, do not attempt any of these pranks on any man, woman, child, or beast.

TEXT COPYRIGHT © 2015 BY DAN BULLA
ILLUSTRATIONS COPYRIGHT © 2015 ETHAN RILLY

LIBRARY OF CONGRESS CATALOGING-IN-PUBLICATION DATA AVAILABLE.
ISBN 978-1-4521-4305-7

MANUFACTURED IN CHINA.

FSC
www.fsc.org
MIX
Paper from
responsible sources
FSC™ C016973

DESIGN BY MICHAEL MORRIS

CHRONICLE BOOKS LLC
680 SECOND STREET
SAN FRANCISCO, CA 94107
WWW.CHRONICLEBOOKS.COM

10 9 8 7 6 5 4 3 2 1

TO DROLL PRANKSTERS EVERYWHERE.

DEAR READER,

I have seen the world and tasted of its many pleasures. I have been entertained by every form of entertainment, diverted by every diversion, and amused by every amusement. And I tell you truly—nothing in this world can quite compare with the joy of pranking rich boys.

In the pages that follow, I assure you that you will find only the finest, drollest pranks. Each and every one of them has been tested on at least three (3) rich boys, and they worked admirably in every case.

Why rich boys, you ask? I suppose it's simply because they take disappointment so badly! They pout and mope and throw fussy little tantrums. And besides, the higher the pedestal, the more fun it is to knock someone off of it!

Go, therefore! There is a world full of rich boys just waiting to be pranked. Let this trusty little tome guide you as you poke them, prod them, tweak and torment them!

I wish you well, and leave you with the Prankster's Blessing: May you always be the one to make the joke, and never be the butt!

Yours in Mischief,

THE DROLL PRANKSTER

Put a shot of espresso in another fellow's morning tea. You
will ensure that the poor chap's day gets
off to a shaky start!

Sew up the lapel on another fellow's blazer.
The poor chap will be forced to carry his boutonnière in his
hand, like a fool!

Put Xs and Os at the bottom of another fellow's letter.
His friends will think he closes his missives with hugs
and kisses, like a lovesick schoolgirl!

Intercept another fellow's invitations, and white out the SVPs
of his RSVPs. His guests-to-be will think him the rudest of
fellows when they see the command, *"Répondez!"*

Dull the blade of another fellow's letter opener. You will rejoice as the defeated fellow cries himself to sleep on top of a pile of unopened letters.

Sew a pocket on the front of another fellow's favorite shirt. The poor fellow will look like he's wearing a common workman's blouse!

Raise the bottom hem on another fellow's running shorts. When he performs his jumping jacks, the poor chap's friends will catch a glimpse of the family jewels!

Replace another fellow's double-breasted suit with a triple-breasted suit. You will delight in the poor fellow's humiliation when he is mocked for his extra breast!

Place binoculars in another fellow's bedroom. His friends will think he spies on his neighbors, like a peeping Thomas!

Install clashing window treatments in another fellow's boudoir. You will rejoice in his humiliation when his friends discover that the curtains do not match the drapes!

Make another fellow's bed, and tuck the sheets so tightly that he is unable to get in. The poor fellow will be forced to nap on top of the covers, like a common drunkard!

Introduce the common ground squirrel to another fellow's island. The poor chap will come to be known as "the Lord of Squirrel Island."

Drop a skinny rabbit in another fellow's garden.
By nightfall, the poor fellow will be distraught,
and the rabbit will be fat and happy!

———·———

Place a heron's nest beside another fellow's koi pond. By
week's end, the poor chap will be left with nothing but an
empty pond and a host of heavyset herons!

Replace another fellow's guard dogs with gentle Swiss hug-hounds. The poor fellow's intruders will be greeted with exuberant puppy kisses!

Remove the proudest feather from another fellow's cap and replace it with the feather of a lesser bird.

Replace another fellow's top hat with a pork pie hat. You will delight in his shame as the poor chap skulks around town in his insufficiently-tall headpiece.

Add one more corner to another fellow's vintage tri-cornered hat. You will rejoice as the poor fellow is roundly mocked for his stupid square hat.

Shave down the tines on another fellow's dinner forks until they are indistinguishable from salad forks. His dinner guests will be perplexed!

Discreetly remove another fellow's napkin from his food sack. Later, you will delight in his shame as he sups like a barbarian.

— ◆ —

Switch around another fellow's aperitifs and digestifs. The poor chap will feel full before eating a single bite, but after dinner is over, he'll develop quite an appetite!

Teach another fellow's monkey butler several bawdy jokes. At his next dinner party, the ribald monkey jokester will shame his poor master!

Steal another fellow's chamber pot. When nature calls in the dead of night, the poor fellow will literally be left without a pot to piss in.

Train your hounds to empty their bowels in another fellow's moat. In time, the poor chap's estate will be surrounded by a river of dung!

Put single-ply toilet tissue in another fellow's lavatory. On his next visit to the loo, the poor buffoon will be in for a rough surprise!

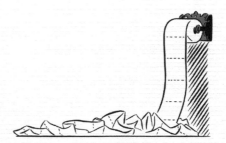

Add extra sand to another fellow's hourglass.
You will rejoice as the poor fool sits in his study all
day, whiling away the hours.

Sew up the fob on another fellow's waistcoat. He will be forced to wear his timepiece on his wrist, like a refuse collector!

Replace another fellow's sundial with one calibrated for a different latitude. The poor dupe will ask to sup mid-afternoon, like a fool!

Cut a hole in another fellow's butterfly net. You will delight in his exasperation as he blunders through the garden, whiffing at monarchs.

Loose a parasite on another fellow's apple orchard. Come autumn, he will despair at the low quality of his cider!

Replace another fellow's ladybugs with promiscuous French floozy-bugs. On his next stroll through the garden, the poor chap will be overwhelmed by a swarm of unladylike pests!

Set a colony of termites upon another fellow's ship in a bottle.
After they have wreaked their havoc, the poor fellow will have
nothing left but a bottle full of bugs.

Steal another fellow's milk. The poor chap will be forced to eat his cookies undunked, like a street urchin!

Make a volcano out of another fellow's mashed
potatoes. His dinner guests will erupt with laughter
when they see that the poor chap plays with his food,
like a simpleton!

Hide another fellow's soup spoons. At dinner, the poor chap
will be forced to slurp soup straight from the bowl, like a
vagabond!

Alter another fellow's portrait so that his hand
is not in his jacket, but in the waistband
of his pants like a common pervert!

Run another fellow's priceless Flemish tapestries through a washing machine. When he sees them swishing round and round, the poor chap will be in a spin!

Stand in the background while another fellow's portrait is painted. The poor chap's painting will be sabotaged by your "portrait bomb."

Chisel down the private parts on another fellow's statue.
You will delight in the poor fellow's shame when his friends
mock his tiny marble manhood!

Put food wrappings in the backseat of another fellow's automobile. Proclaim that the only title the poor fellow deserves is that of "burger king."

———◆———

Put a pinch of sand in another fellow's driving gloves. The next time he drives, the poor chap will be even more uncomfortable than the man who drives barehanded!

Tamper with the horn on another fellow's automobile. The next time the poor chap gives it a honk, his sabotaged vehicle will play a traditional Mexican folk song!

Add gutters and walls to another fellow's "infinity pool." His guests will feel no sense of awe as they splash around his sad, finite pool.

Install a barbecue-grill in another fellow's backyard. The poor chap's neighbors will think he cooks his food over an open flame, like a caveman!

———— · ————

Skip stones across another fellow's tranquility pond. You will delight in the poor chap's disquietude as he reflects upon the agitated waters.

Hire a landscape architect to alter another fellow's garden maze. The next time he goes for a stroll, the poor fellow will be lost in his own labyrinth!

Glue another fellow's wine bottles inside of brown paper bags. When he presents his most-prized vintage at dinner, the poor chap will look like a destitute street wino!

Give another fellow a faulty decanter. You will rejoice as the poor dupe suffocates his finest wines!

Heed the call of nature in another fellow's vineyard. Next year, his pinot will taste like pee, no?

Before dinner, place a "whoopee" balloon on another fellow's seat. The flatulent fellow will be escorted from supper in disgrace!

Spread a rumor that another fellow's family motto is "*Dum spiro pedo*"—"While I breathe, I break wind." His friends will have a gas at the expense of the gassy fellow!

Over-tighten the lacing on another fellow's corset.
You will delight in the poor chap's wheezing and rejoice
in his heaving bosom!

Apply a layer of dust to another fellow's Japanese folding
fan. As he fans his face with dusty air, the poor chap will walk
around batting his eyelashes like a shameless flirt!

Fill another fellow's dictionary with erroneous spellings. You will delight in his shame as he mixes up his letters, like a bumbler at a spelling bee!

Replace a handful of iambs with dactyls in another fellow's sonnet. The poor fellow's beloved will be put off by his clumsy verse!

———⟨◆⟩———

Take another fellow's Latin exam and replace all instances of the dative with the vocative. The poor chap will appear to be confounded by Latin declension!

Remove the bow ties from another fellow's costumed pigs. Their choreographed dances will henceforth be less delightful.

Steal another fellow's tie clip. The poor chap
will be forced to walk around with his tie swinging freely,
like a common gigolo!

———— ·· ————

Rub dirt on another fellow's necktie. Before he has a chance
to clean it, announce that the poor chap has soiled his ascot!

Move the bow from another fellow's forefinger to his middle finger. The poor chap will forget the thing he wanted to remember, and remember the thing he wanted to forget!

Seal off another fellow's cloakroom. At his next dinner party, the poor chap will be forced to pile his guest's cloaks on top of a bed, like a coatroom in a brothel.

———————

Tie-dye another fellow's blazer. You will delight in his shame when the poor chap is mocked for his coat of many colors!

Remove the epaulettes from another fellow's coat. You will exult in the humiliated fellow's unadorned shoulders!

Give another fellow a Champagne bottle made from plexiglass. When he tries to christen his ship, the bottle will bounce into the sea!

Crack the bottom glasses in another fellow's Champagne tower. You will rejoice when the bubbly chap's Champagne waterfall becomes a Champagne flood!

Spike the punch at another fellow's party. As he stumbles around the ballroom like a concussed boxer, suggest that the poor fellow is punch drunk!

Steal another fellow's saucers. When he next takes his tea, the poor chap will be forced to carry his teacup in his hand, like a common oaf!

Sprinkle another fellow's gunpowder into his smoking pipe. The next time he indulges in a puff of tobacco, the poor fellow will be hoisted by his own petard!

Prick a tiny hole in another fellow's ear lobe. His friends will think the poor chap pierces his ears, like an opium merchant!

Replace another fellow's chewing tobacco with chewing gum. His associates will shun the smacking fellow, thinking that he consorts with gum chewers!

Replace another fellow's masseuse with a Swedish tickling expert. After his next session, the poor chap will literally be tickled pink!

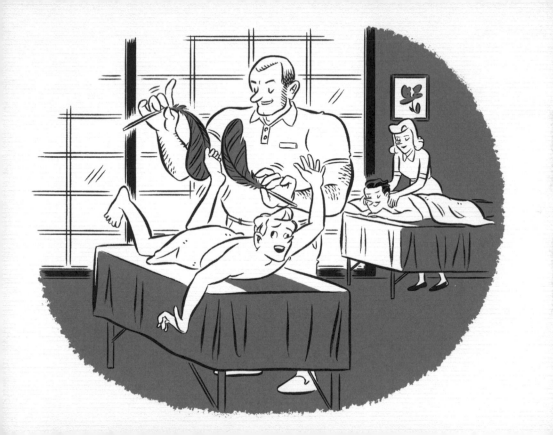

Steal another fellow's parasol. After his next
noonday stroll, the poor fellow's sun-kissed cheeks
will be as pink as a farmer's!

Replace another fellow's spectacles with Italian sun-spectacles. The poor buffoon will be forced to wear his tinted glasses indoors, like a cinema star!

***

Put another fellow's Swiss chocolate in the sun. By the end of the day, the poor chap will be left with nothing but a puddle of hot cocoa!

Attach horseshoes to the bottom of another fellow's loafers. His friends will be vexed as the poor chap hoofs about, clicking and clacking like a song and dance man!

———

Give another fellow a saddle that has too wide of a twist. When he next goes riding, you will delight in the poor fellow's chafed thighs.

Replace another fellow's pony with a bucking bronco. You will rejoice as the poor chap is tossed about, like a rodeo star!

Hide small weights in another fellow's ballet slippers. At his next recital, the lumbering clod will be mocked for his oafish *pointe* work.

Replace the penny in another fellow's loafers with a Mexican peso coin. Henceforth, greet him with "*hola*," which is Mexican for "hello."

———

Put an extra argyle stocking in another fellow's dryer. The poor chap will think he has one stocking too few, when really he has one stocking too many!

Put a lump of coal in another fellow's Christmas sock.
The poor fellow's Christmas will be spent in despair, as he
wonders what he did to deserve a place on the naughty list!

Steal another fellow's underarm powder. You will exult in the rank chap's undeodorized pits!

———— ⟨⟩ ————

Replace another fellow's agarwood incense with sulfur sticks. When the poor fellow lights them aflame, the stench will leave him incensed!

Cross-breed another fellow's roses with the Brazilian stink flower. Come mid-spring, the poor chap will be in for a malodorous surprise!

Place trick candles on another fellow's birthday cake.
As the despondent fellow huffs and puffs,
you will delight in his unfulfilled wishes.

Put roman candles in another fellow's candelabra.
The next time the poor chap tries to set the mood,
he'll set off a fireworks show instead!

Punch a hole in another fellow's bellows. The poor chap will pump at the broken device in vain as he quivers before his feeble fire!

———————

Add additional hot stones to another fellow's sauna. You will delight in his discomfort as the poor chap sweats like a summertime hog!

Steal another fellow's crumb scrapers. After his next meal, the poor fellow will have to scrape away the table crumbs with his hand, like a common brute!

———— ❧ ————

Overtorch the top layer of another fellow's crème brûlée. When he taps on the rock-hard caramel, the only thing the poor chap will crack will be his spoon!

Remove the fortune from another fellow's fortune cookie.
The poor chap will eat his empty cookie in despair, thinking
that the future holds nothing for him!

Knock another fellow's piano slightly out of tune.
At his next cocktail party, the poor fellow's salon
will sound more like a saloon!

Steal another fellow's cufflink collection. The poor fellow
will be forced to fasten his cuffs with buttons, like a
rock and roll musician!

Remove the clapper from the inside of another fellow's bell.
You will delight in the poor chap's hollow efforts to summon
his butler, as he shakes his empty bell like a madman!

Introduce a smattering of superfluous sharps and flats into another fellow's sheet music. His recital will be a humiliating affair!

Put a picture of a chimp in another fellow's locket. When the poor chap tries to show off his beloved, he will appear to be a seducer of apes!

Replace another fellow's swan with an ugly duckling. The next time he strolls around his pond, the poor fellow will be startled by the hideous feathered freak!

Shave the mane off another fellow's lion. The poor chap will find that his "king of the jungle" is nothing more than a sad, bald beast!

Dismantle the motor on another fellow's carousel.
The poor chap will be shamed by the stationary horses
on his merry-go-nowhere.

Train another fellow's dressage horse to do the salsa. The other equestrians will ostracize the poor chap when they see his horse's dirty dancing!

———— ◆ ————

Shrink another fellow's horse riding breeches. The next time he goes out for a trot, the poor fellow will be forced to ride sidesaddle, like a pastor's wife!

Put spurs on the back of another fellow's Wellingtons.
People will think the poor chap is a patron of
honky tonks and a champion of the do-si-do!

Slightly raise the nets on another fellow's tennis courts. The poor fellow's next tennis performance will be a comedy of unforced errors!

Oil the soles of another fellow's lawn bowling shoes. After the poor oaf slips three times, call him a turkey!

———

Warp the wood on another fellow's pool cue. When he mis-hits the cue ball, suggest that perhaps the poor chap's billiards play is not "up to scratch."

Cut the collar off another fellow's turtleneck sweater. You will rejoice as the shell-shocked chap is mocked for his fleshy, naked neck!

※

Sew up the ends of another fellow's muff. The shivering fellow will be forced to walk around with his hands in his pockets, like a country bumpkin!

Put a family of beavers in another fellow's Swiss chalet. On his next trip to the mountains, the poor chap will find nothing but an empty plot of land and a bevy of engorged beavers.

Loosen the blades on another fellow's ice skates. When the poor oaf slips and falls, christen him with the nickname "quadruple klutz."

Square off the sides of another fellow's ice spheres. His friends will think the poor chap cubes his ice, like a housewife!

———◈———

Cut the cord on another fellow's ice box. When the poor fellow goes looking for his evening iced cream, he will find nothing but a tub of warm milk!

Dump salt on another fellow's ice sculptures.
The poor chap will watch in horror as his winter gala
turns into a slushy soiree!

Replace another fellow's fainting couch with a bean bag chair. His friends will think the poor chap lounges on a bag of beans, like a coffee farmer!

———— ◆ ————

Mount rockers on the bottom of another fellow's favorite chair. When he next sits down, the startled chap will rock to and fro, like an oaf in a rowboat!

Replace the club chair in another fellow's study with a recliner. You will rejoice when the poor chap earns the humiliating moniker "La-Z-Man."

Replace another fellow's polo mallet with a gavel. You will rejoice as the poor chap rides around wildly, swinging his tiny mallet like a judge gone mad!

Put bedsheets with a slightly lower thread count on another fellow's bed. You will delight in the addled fellow's fitful slumbers.

ACKNOWLEDGMENTS

Thank you to Wynn Rankin, Michael Morris, Ethan Rilly and everyone at Chronicle Books for your passion and enthusiasm for this project.

Thank you to Emily, Jenny, Jim, and Susan Bulla, for your love and support.

Many thanks to Stan Q. Wash, Kassie Couey, Jasbir Singh Vazquez, Connor Tillman, the Kistlers, and the Pattersons. And an extra special thanks to Carol Gillard, without whom this book would not exist.

Lastly, thank you to the Tumblr community for all of your support. You can find more Droll Pranks at www.drollpranks.tumblr.com, or on Twitter at @drollpranks.

ABOUT THE AUTHOR

Dan Bulla is a writer and comedian from Chicago, living in Los Angeles. He is a regular performer at the iO West Theater in Hollywood and a contributor to the Onion News Network. Whenever he has time to spare, he occupies himself with droll matters.